I0012128

Blox Fruits Dark Coat, Devils Fruit and Buddha Game guide

Tips and tricks to navigate the game

Daniel A. Daniels

Table of contents

Why This Blox Fruits Guide: Your Navigation System on the High Seas

The salty spray hurts your face, the wind rips through your sails, and a swarm of seagulls shouts above you. You're at the helm of your ship, clutching a chart in your sweating palm, but the island you're looking for is covered in mist. Blox Fruits is a wide ocean of adventure where pirates of all kinds carve their fortunes amid clashing steel and exotic talents. Beyond the excitement of fighting and the allure of gold, however, comes a terrifying truth: navigating these unexplored seas is not for the faint of heart. This is when this tutorial comes in handy. Consider it a combination of your trusted sextant, worn logbook, and seasoned first mate. You'll discover the information, methods, and secrets you need to navigate the hazardous currents of Blox Fruits and carve your legacy as a pirate to be reckoned with inside these pages.

Exploring the Unknown Depths:
Blox Fruits is much more than a button-mashing fight. It's a world full of complicated dynamics, hidden synergies, and hidden Easter eggs. This guide delves deep into the game's heart, studying every battle style, examining Devil Fruit power sets, and uncovering the complexities of island exploration and resource management. You'll learn how to maximize the potential of your chosen combat style, execute deadly combinations, and strategically use wicked Fruit powers.

Mapping Your Path to Mastery:
Blox Fruits leveling is more than simply mindless grinding. This article provides effective tactics for increasing your XP gain, whether via clever island hopping, spectacular boss encounters, or joining up with other pirates for daring raids. You'll uncover secret grinding places, learn to exploit enemy vulnerabilities, and unlock tactics that will allow you to alter the tide of combat even against the most difficult opponents.

From Scoundrel to Savant at Sea:
Blox Fruits is about more than just raw power; it's also about wit and ingenuity. This book will teach you how to be a clever trader by negotiating advantageous agreements, learning the art of bartering, and spotting profitable market trends. You'll discover how to use your knowledge of hidden riches, rare minerals, and strong Devil Fruits to create a wealth that would make even the most greedy pirate captain green with envy.

Beyond the Fundamentals: Your Pass to Legendary Status:
This guide does not end at the surface. It digs into the sophisticated skills and secrets that distinguish great pirates from legends. You'll discover secret boss battles, master the art of PvP combat, discover the cryptic Dark Coat, and even discover the intriguing power of the Buddha fighting style. You'll uncover new depths to your talents with each page, pushing the limits of Blox Fruits and carving your name into the game's hall of fame.

Not Just a Guide, But a Community:
This isn't a sterile, frigid handbook. It's a link that connects you to the thriving Blox Fruits community. You'll discover tips and methods drawn from the collective knowledge of veteran gamers, humorous accounts of epic adventures, and even challenges and dares to test your mettle and feed your feeling of camaraderie inside these pages. Remember that the pirate life is best lived alongside other swashbucklers!

A Journey, Not a Place:
Finally, this book is an invitation to explore rather than a tool to conquer. Blox Fruits is a dynamic, breathing world that is always adding new material, puzzles, and mysteries. This tutorial provides the groundwork, piques your interest, and prepares you to adapt and succeed when the game throws new challenges your way. Remember that the actual fun of Blox Fruits is found in the discovery, experimenting, and exhilaration of crafting your own unique tale on the broad open seas.

Cast off the lines, hoist the Jolly Roger, and use this guidance as a compass as you set sail on your epic Blox Fruits adventure. Remember that the best riches aren't necessarily money and diamonds; they're the memories produced in the flames of adventure, the relationships formed with fellow pirates, and the joy of conquering apparently impossible obstacles. You're not simply sailing the seas with this guide at your side; you're creating your own pirate mythology, one daring accomplishment at a time.

Set sail, courageous explorer, and may the wind always be at your back

Introduction

Welcome aboard, Buccaneers! Hello and welcome to Your Blox Fruits Odyssey!

The salty spray tickles your nose, the wind whispers secrets in your ear, and the setting sun paints the horizon in pirate-worthy gold tones. You're standing on the deck of your trusted ship, your pulse pumping with the excitement of adventure, yet a knot of doubt pulls at your belly. Blox Fruits beckons, its huge archipelago glistening with both promise and hazard. Devil Fruits throb with mystical power, swords clash in ferocious dances, and fabled riches lay buried under sun-dried sands. However, the route to pirate fame is perilous, cloaked in fog and rife with perils. Don't worry, fellow buccaneer! "The Blox Fruits Odyssey: Your Guide to Pirate Legend" serves as your compass, first mate, and treasure map all in one. These pages reveal not just techniques and mechanics, but also the core spirit of Blox Fruits. You'll discover the mysteries of Devil Fruits and use surgical precision to unleash their destructive power. With each perfectly timed combination, you'll master the art of battle, etching your name into the legend. You'll become an astute trader, acquiring wealth that would strangle the Kraken's tentacles. Beyond the fundamentals, you'll uncover hidden depths, secret challenges, and legendary Easter eggs that will etch your name in the hall of the most daring pirates in Blox Fruits. This is more than a guide; it is an invitation. An invitation to join a thriving community of swashbucklers, exchange accounts of heroic fights and narrow escapes, and put your skills to the test against your fellow adventurers. It's an invitation to explore, experiment, push the limits of what's possible, and construct your own distinct tale on the high seas. This Odyssey offers something for everyone, whether you're a seasoned sea dog or a fresh-faced cabin boy. Whether you seek the rush of PvP battle, the pleasure of mastering a fighting style, or the cunning thrill of the market, the secret to unleashing your real pirate potential lies inside these pages.

Cast off the lines, spread your sails, and let "The Blox Fruits Odyssey" take you on your biggest voyage yet. Remember that the pirate life is about more than simply plunder and glory; it's about the voyage, the friendships, and the tales you make along the way. You're not simply sailing the seas with this guide at your side; you're authoring your own tale, one epic chapter at a time.

Allow the journey to begin!

Part 1: Learning the Fundamentals

Thank you for visiting Blox Fruits:
As you clutch the helm of your tiny raft, a rickety vessel carrying your pirate fantasies, the salty spray sears your skin. Blox Fruits is a massive open world Roblox adventure in which you'll cruise the broad seas, explore secret islands, learn legendary combat techniques, and, of course, eat Devil Fruits to gain astonishing abilities. But, before you channel your inner Luffy, let's take the initial steps on your quest.

Character Development and Progression:
Your adventure starts with the creation of your avatar. Choose from a variety of races, each with its own set of stat advantages and visual distinctions. Then comes the most important decision: your fighting style. Fist Fighting epitomizes raw force and combinations, while Swordsmanship provides accuracy and ranged assaults. Axeman specializes on raw power and area-of-effect strikes, while Gunslinger specializes in long-range supremacy with

specialized guns. Each design appeals to a particular kind of playstyle, so explore to discover the one that speaks to your inner pirate. Leveling up allows you to realize your full potential. The universe throws challenges to you: tasks to accomplish, foes to defeat, and monsters to defeat. Each win grants you Beli, the main money, as well as experience points, which fill your bar. Reaching a new level increases your basic stats, making you stronger, tougher, and more prepared to face harder opponents. However, leveling involves more than simply raw power. Points may be allocated to three essential stats: Strength improves attack power, Defense improves health and resistance, and Agility improves movement speed and dodge probability. Understanding and mastering stat optimization becomes critical for conquering subsequent tasks.

Exploring the World:
The huge archipelago of Blox Fruits invites exploration with a ship beneath your feet and wind in your sails. Each island has its own atmosphere, adversaries, and secrets. First Sea, your starting island, acts as a training ground.

The courageous pirates then set off toward the Second Sea, a country of searing deserts and old temples. The Third Sea entices with its perilous volcanic vistas and fearsome monsters. Beyond the horizon lies the legendary New World, shrouded in mystery and packed with unrivaled challenges and incredible riches. But sailing isn't always a piece of cake. The wide seas are fraught with peril. Sea Kings, huge leviathans, emerge from the depths to destroy your ship. Sharks circle for a taste of fresh pirate, while krakens lurk in the depths, ready to pull you and your ship to their doom. Navigating these dangers requires care, alertness, and maybe a well-placed cannon blast or two.

Basic Combat Skills:
Now comes the most important part of each pirate's life: battle! It is critical to master basic attacks. Your left click initiates a regular punch or sword swing, and your right click initiates a more powerful, slower strike. Learn to connect these moves together into combinations for tremendous harm. Dodging is your only hope. Timed spacebar pushes let you to avoid opponent punches, leaving them vulnerable to

counterattacks. Don't forget about blocking! Holding the E key increases your defense, repelling lesser strikes and allowing you time to plot your next move.

Fruity Treats:
The Devil Fruit, mysterious orbs that provide exceptional abilities in return for the ability to swim, is one of Blox Fruit's distinguishing elements. Each fruit has a different power, such as launching scorching meteors or teleporting across the battlefield. Logia fruits give elemental mastery, while Paramecia fruits concentrate on utility and manipulation. Zoan fruits convert you into formidable monsters, each with its unique set of advantages and disadvantages. Choosing the correct Devil Fruit may have a huge impact on your playstyle and fighting strategy. Experiment with them, put them to the test, and find the fruit that speaks to your inner pirate.

Dark Coat Tips:
The Dark Coat is a road to power that lies beyond the Devil Fruits. This enigmatic clothing is cloaked in mystery, revealed via

hidden challenges and delivering a distinct fighting style that combines swordsmanship, sorcery, and darkness. The Dark Coat needs agility and timing to master. Its actions alternate between attacking and defensive blows, rewarding flawless combinations and penalizing reckless aggressiveness. It takes effort to unlock the coat's full potential, but mastery gives incredible strength and adaptability, making you a force to be reckoned with on any battlefield.

The Buddha's Path:

The Buddha fighting technique appeals to individuals seeking inner calm as well as lethal strength. This ancient discipline exemplifies both attacking and defensive strength. When Buddha moves, he unleashes tremendous fists and kicks that may shake the ground and shatter through foes. But the Buddha isn't just about force. Its expertise is based on its defensive abilities. Healing procedures replenish your health, while buffs and shields increase your resistance. The Buddha provides a unique playstyle that depends on controlled aggressiveness and unflinching tenacity while balancing offensive and defense. This is just the beginning of your Blox Fruits adventure. With a good grip on the fundamentals, you're ready to

set sail and put your skills to the test in warfare.

Part 2: Advanced Strategies and Techniques

Mastering the Art of Grinding: Earning Your Sea Legs Through Sweat and Steel
Leveling up in Blox Fruits is about more than simply bragging rights; it unlocks new talents, increases stats, and opens the door to more difficult tasks. But who wants to waste hours pummeling the same old crabs? Here are some effective methods for turning the grind into a thrill

Daily Rituals: The value of consistency should not be underestimated. Completing daily tasks on a regular basis gives a continuous flow of experience and Beli, putting you on the correct track.

Island Hopping Safari: Approach each island as a distinct hunting zone. Islands with higher-leveled species provide more experience benefits, but keep in mind that danger and reward go hand in hand. Plan your expeditions carefully and be prepared to flee if the local animals greets you with open claws.

Boss Blitz with Friends: Challenging bosses aren't simply treasure pinatas; they're XP goldmines as well. Joining up with other pirates for boss raids increases your firepower and spreads the danger. Coordination your strikes, use support skills, and watch your experience bar soar.

Optimized Grinding Spots: Enemies swarm like ants on a picnic blanket in some secret nooks or forgotten lanes. These "grinding spots" provide focused XP farming, but the repetition may be overwhelming. To keep things interesting, switch up the places, try out new combinations, and create personal mini-challenges.

From Novice to Nemesis: Bossing Around

It's not just about sheer power when it comes to bosses; it's a tactical dance of preparation, awareness, and deliberate assault. Here's how to transform boss battles into enjoyable tests of ability rather than hair-tearing wrath fests:

Know Your Enemy: Don't go into a boss battle unprepared. Investigate their assault patterns, find vulnerabilities, and comprehend their distinct dynamics. Some bosses penalize button mashers, while others demand patient baiting and counterattacks.

Get Ready for Glory: Don't try to put out a fire with a damp paper towel. Equip weapons and equipment that are targeted to the boss's weaknesses. A flaming sword against a water-based giant will almost certainly result in a watery demise.

Combo King & Queen: Chain your most powerful strikes together for maximum damage output during boss battles. Experiment with various combinations, practice timing, and learn to release your rage at the appropriate times.

Teamwork is Required to Make the Dream Come True: Some bosses make fun of solitary explorers. Gathering a crew is critical for these giants. Assign responsibilities, use healing and support skills, and plan your assaults as if you were a well-oiled pirate machine.

PvP Abilities: Dominating the Arena with Style
The salty spray does not provide consolation to all pirates. Some people yearn for the clash of steel against steel, the pleasure of outwitting their opponents in the crucible of PvP. Here are

some pointers to help you go from novice swashbuckler to arena legend:

Master Your Craft: Improve your knowledge of your chosen combat technique. Learn advanced tactics, practice combinations, and improve your overall battle flow. A swordsman who just uses basic cuts is begging to be parried into obscurity.

Adapt and Respond: Don't become a known target. Learn to anticipate your opponent's actions, change your strategy on the fly, and exploit their flaws. A well-timed parry may alter the tide of combat.

Fruit Fusion: In PvP, some Devil Fruits and fighting style benefits shine. Experiment to discover the setting that gives you the advantage. A well-timed Smoker "White Death" may paralyze an aggressive brawler.

Practice Makes Perfect: Sharpen your talents by competing against other players, even if you lose at first. Each encounter teaches you something new and helps you improve your PvP strategies. Even the most experienced pirates had to learn to walk the plank before they could rule the seas.

From Scoundrel to Scourge: Bounty Hunting
Take up bounty hunting to become the terror of the wide sea and collect the benefits. Find wanted pirates, vanquish them in fight, and collect their bounty for large Beli prizes. But keep in mind that seeking high-level bounties takes considerable power, ingenuity, and a fair dose of prudence.

Hunt Smarter, Not Harder: Do your homework before setting sail. High-level bounty hunters often specialize on certain prey, leveraging their hunting grounds expertise and favored techniques.

Follow Like a Hawk: To locate your quarry, use in-game tools such as Bounty Boards and community information. Tracking abilities and deductive reasoning skills might lead you to unwary pirates lurking in plain sight.

Come Together for the Thrill: A well-coordinated team might be your most valuable asset when it comes to infamous bounties. To bring down the enemy, divide and conquer, use crowd control techniques, and unleash deadly combinations.Even the most infamous pirates. Remember that collaboration is what makes the dream come true, particularly when it entails collecting a large reward and bragging rights in the local bar.

How to Trade: From Barter to Bonanza

Blox Fruits is more than just a site for headbutting and looting; it's also a busy marketplace where clever pirates can convert a Beli into a fortune. Here are some pointers to help you navigate the perilous seas of trade:

Knowledge is Strength: Don't get into the market blindly. Investigate item values, comprehend demand patterns, and be wary of possible frauds. Paying too much for a rusted sword will make you poorer and wiser, but not in a good way.

Bargain Like a Kraken: Remember that bargaining is an art form. Practice your negotiating abilities, be ready to walk away, and don't be scared to counteroffer. A sharp tongue may often get you the greatest discounts.

Diversify for Success: Concentrating on certain things or resources will help you attract consumers who are seeking for your expertise. Become the island's go-to provider of swordsmen, the expert in rare Devil Fruit knowledge, or the vendor of uncommon manufacturing materials. Niche markets may be very profitable.

Bundles of Joy: Offer bundles or discounts for large orders. It not only attracts customers, but it also frees up inventory space, allowing you to reinvest your Beli in larger fish. Remember that satisfied consumers are likely to return.

Secret Techniques: Discovering Hidden Wonders

Blox Fruits is full of hidden mysteries and Easter eggs just waiting to be found. Some provide substantial benefits, while others merely lend a sense of mystery and pleasure to your quest. Keep your eyes open and examine every place; you never know what gems you could find:

Wall Hacks (Not These): Certain islands' walls may look solid, yet a well-placed sword swipe might expose hidden corridors or secret apartments. Experiment and explore to find yourself swimming in treasure or unlocking special tasks.

In the Wind Whispers: Pay great attention to landmarks, especially old ruins or secret shrines. The wind may sometimes carry whispers of forgotten secrets or hints to hidden obstacles. Understanding these whispers may lead to strong improvements or hidden prizes.

Fruitful Fusion: Some Devil Fruits give unique advantages or unleash secret powers when consumed in a precise sequence. Experimenting with various combinations might result in deadly new abilities or surprising benefits. Remember that education is the most valuable money in Blox Fruits!

Musical Enigmas: Certain islands have musical puzzles in which particular notes on instruments open secret entrances or trigger helpful benefits. Sharpen your ear and channel your inner bard; the tunes may contain the key to revealing long-lost mysteries.

Remember, when it comes to learning the advanced tactics and strategies in Blox Fruits, this is only the top of the iceberg. Experimentation, practice, and adaptability are essential for realizing the game's full potential. And remember to have fun! On the huge seas of Blox Fruits, explore, conquer, and become the legend you were born to be.

Stay tuned for Part 3, in which we go into detailed guidelines for Devil Fruits, the Dark Coat, and the Buddha combat style. We'll study great combinations, uncover their hidden potential, and arm you with the knowledge to unleash their real power on your foes.
The journey continues!

Part 3: In-Depth Guides

Your Devil Fruit Compendium: Unleashing the Fury

Blox Fruits' Devil Fruits are more than just tempting nibbles; they're keys to unleashing incredible abilities. However, with more than 30 fruits to pick from, navigating this sea of skills may be difficult. This book acts as a compass, digging into the unique qualities, awakenings, and combination possibilities of each fruit to assist you in selecting the right one to carve your tale.

Paramecia Authority:

Gum-Gum Fruit: Luffy's famous fruit has elastic limbs and comical mechanics, making it ideal for close-combat brawlers. Learn "Gum-Gum Pistol" and "Gum-Gum Rocket" combinations for destructive punches and aerial assaults. Awakening grants access to Gear forms, which provide additional power enhancements.

Chop-Chop Fruit: Kizaru's fruit grants your body superhuman speed, making it suitable for sword-wielding adventurers. Use lightning-fast slashes and teleporting moves like "Yata no Kagami" to gain unrivaled mobility and attacking capability. You can control and manipulate light after awakening.

Smoke-Smoke Fruit: Smoker's fruit turns you into a cloud of smoke, giving you excellent evading abilities as well as strong area-of-effect strikes like "White Death" and "White Smoke Mashi." Awakening improves smoke manipulation and grants access to destructive air-based methods.

Logia Expertise:

Ace's flaming fruit allows you to manipulate and release flames, making it ideal for long-range assaults and battlefield supremacy. Use combinations like "Great Fireball" and "Crimson Lotus: Ace" to wreak havoc. Awakening increases your ability to manipulate fire and unlocks fiery transformations.

Sand-Sand Fruit: The desert ability of Crocodile lets you manipulate and become sand, providing amazing resistance and deadly ground-based attacks such as "Sables: Pestilence" and "Desert Grande Espada."

Awakening offers control over sand and allows you to manipulate the ground.

Ice-Ice Fruit: Aokiji's ice fruit allows you to freeze the environment around you, allowing you to manage crowds and defend yourself. Use combinations like "Ice Time" and "Blizzard" to perform chilling assaults and manipulate the battlefield. Awakening improves ice manipulation and grants access to freezing auras.

Zoan Conversions:

Phoenix Fruit: Marco's fabled fruit bestows phoenix-like abilities such as regeneration, fire manipulation, and aerial prowess. Learn combinations like "Blue Bird" and "Rebirth" for powerful assaults and healing. Awakening grants complete phoenix metamorphosis and increased regeneration.

Rumble Rumble Fruit: Enel's mythological fruit charges you with energy, allowing you to unleash deadly lightning strikes and area-of-effect attacks such as "Raigo" and "El Thor." Awakening improves your control over electricity and enables transformations for more mobility and power.

Giraffe Fruit: Kaku's zoan fruit turns you into a colossal giraffe, offering you long-range strikes and strong kicks like "Giraffero Gun" and "Giraffero Stamp." Awakening improves your giraffe form, allowing you to grow in size and attack strength.

The Dark Coat Guide to Unlocking Hidden Potential

The Dark Coat is more than simply a fashionable outfit; it's a doorway to unique fighting tactics and darkness mastery. This tutorial dissects every facet of the Dark Coat, enabling you to maximize its combat potential:

Principles and Techniques:

Shadow Claw: Your primary attack, striking with a shadowy claw strike. Learn how to combine it into combinations for more damage and smoothness.

Dark gateway: Construct a dark gateway that allows you to travel short distances for evasive maneuvers or surprise strikes. For tactical advantage, master its timing and location.

Grim Blast: Release a barrage of shadow punches, ideal for piercing opponent defenses and causing prolonged damage. To maximize its efficacy, practice its rhythmic flow.

Advanced Combos and Techniques:
Umbral Assault: Charge forward with a strong black slash, perfect for starting battle or closing gaps. When combined with Shadow Claw, it creates a powerful lunge strike.
Void Tendril: Summon a dark tentacle from the earth and smash opponents for tremendous AoE damage. Master its timing and you'll be able to dominate the crowd.
Eclipse Barrier: Raise a whirling wall of darkness that absorbs incoming strikes and temporarily increases attack strength when released. Time it right to counter opponent attacks and launch a devastating counteroffensive.

Fighting Style Synergy:
Swordsmanship: Use shadow dashes and teleporting strikes to improve your mobility and close-range assaults. Make use of the Dark Coat's defensive qualities to build up opportunities for deadly sword combos.

Fist Fighting: Unleash a barrage of shadow punches and kicks imbued with darkness. Use the Dark Coat's evasion and teleportation abilities to keep moving and overwhelm your opponents.

Gun Slinging: Combine long-range weapon assaults with teleporting strikes and shadow attacks to create a lethal combination....manipulation to allow for surprise attacks and tactical positioning. While reloading or unleashing lethal area-of-effect blows with darkness-enhanced bullets, use the Dark Coat's protective barrier to shield yourself.

Mastering the Buddha's Way: Your Enlightenment Path

The Buddha fighting style is about inner peace and deadly power working in perfect harmony, not just brute force. This book presents the Buddha's teachings, assisting you in transforming your inner serenity into a powerful force:

Primary Movements and Ideas:

Four Deva Kings: Altering your position changes your attacks and gives benefits. The

"Diamond King" delivers powerful blows, whilst the "Anger King" unleashes lethal combos. Learn to change postures easily for tactical fighting adaptability.

Chakra Activation: Use your inner energy to provide temporary benefits like damage enhancements and healing auras. Master time and resource management in order to employ chakras effectively.

Mantras: Reciting ancient verses summons powerful attacks such as the area-of-effect "Roronoa Buddha Palm" and the fatal single-target "Wrath of Vajra." Learn their timing and stance for maximum impact.

Advanced Techniques and Strategies:

Meditative Healing: Use your inner calm to heal yourself and your companions, enabling you to turn the tide of battle with sustained regeneration. Use it while in the "Earth King" posture for greatest healing potential.

Diamond Sutra: Transform into an immovable item that deflects incoming attacks and reflects damage back to your opponent. Time this powerful defensive technique to counter opponent offensives and flip the tables.

When shattered, the Golden Bell Buddha transforms into a glittering golden statue, becoming invulnerable and unleashing a huge shockwave. Use this ultimate talent with caution to survive devastating hits and punish enemies with a holy wrath explosion.

Partnership with Other Elements:
Dark Fruits: Combine the Buddha's protecting abilities with the offensive Devil Fruit abilities. With your inner calm, command the battlefield and launch lethal fruit-powered attacks on helpless opponents.
Brown Coat: Balance the anger of the darkness with the serenity of the Buddha. Distract your opponent with teleporting assaults and shadow manipulation while remaining concentrated and ready to unleash powerful Buddhist methods.
Fighting Methods: Adapt the Buddha's posture changes and chakras to your own preference. Swordsmanship benefits from the Diamond King's power, whereas Fist Fighting thrives amid the Anger King's anger. Find the synergy that best matches your playstyle and maximize your potential.

Part 4: Additional Resources and Frequently Asked Questions

Your Blox Fruits journey has only just started, but the broad ocean seas offer innumerable wonders and mysteries that these guides have yet to reveal. Let's dig into a treasure mine of extra materials and commonly asked questions to assist you navigate the ever-changing terrain and become a really legendary pirate:

Ask the Community: Unravel the Mysteries
No pirate ever crosses the plank by himself! The thriving Blox Fruits community is teeming with seasoned explorers willing to share their expertise and answer your burning questions. Here are some often asked questions and their thoughtful responses:

Q: What is the best Devil Fruit?
There is no one "best" fruit since they all appeal to various playstyles and abilities. Experiment with several fruits to discover one that appeals to you. Before making your ultimate pick,

consider your fighting style, preferred battle range, and desired functionality.

Q: How can I quickly level up?
Daily tasks, boss encounters with allies, and smart island hopping are all effective methods to get experience. Grinding areas may be beneficial, but keep in mind to alter positions and practice combinations to keep things interesting.

Q: I'm having trouble with PvP. Any suggestions?
Master your chosen combat style, react to your opponent's actions, and learn how to efficiently use combos and Devil Fruit powers. Consider forming a practice and strategy group with experienced players.

Q: How can I activate the Dark Coat?
After reaching the Second Sea, go on the Sea Beast Raid. You will get this formidable outfit after defeating the Kraken and completing the following challenges.

Q: What are some of the Blox Fruits' hidden secrets?

Keep an eye out for hidden barriers, listen for hints in the wind, and try out alternative item interactions. Some islands have hidden areas, Easter eggs, and even strong upgrades just waiting to be uncovered.

Bonus: Unlocking the Pirate Lexicon and Overcoming Obstacles

A seasoned pirate not only navigates the perilous waterways, but also the language of the underworld. Let's understand the terminology with our Blox Fruits Glossary to guarantee smooth sailing through discussions and menus:

Acc: Account (your personal login)
Beli: In-game currency used for buying, trading, and bounties
Bounty: Reward granted for defeating wanted pirates
Combo: Stringing together multiple attacks for increased damage
CP: Combat Power, a numerical representation of your strength
DF: Devil Fruit, granting unique powers and weaknesses
EXP: Experience Points, used toFruit Main: A player that favors Devil Fruit powers in battle.
Haki: Powerful aura used for advanced combat techniques

Island Hop: Exploring different islands to find enemies, quests, and resources

KB: Knockback, sending enemies flying with attacks

Ken: Sword mastery skill, enhancing sword-based attacks

Mastery: Reaching the highest level of a fighting style

Mob: Smaller enemies encountered in groups

PVP: Player versus Player combat, testing your skills against others

Raid: High-difficulty group boss fight requiring teamwork

Sea Beast: Powerful creatures encountered in specific locations

Skill: Special abilities learned through leveling up your fighting style

Stat: Attribute like Strength, Agility, or Defense, affecting your overall performance

Sword Main: Player who relies primarily on swordsmanship in combat

Trading: Bartering items and Beli with other players

Upgrade: Enhances your abilities, weapons, or equipment

XP Boost: Item or buff that temporarily increases XP gain

Now that you've mastered the language, it's time to put your skills to the test. Challenges and Achievements beckon, promising not just bragging rights but also priceless rewards:

Overall Storyline: Follow the main missions, uncovering islands, defeating monsters, and solving the Blox Fruits world's secrets. Conquer each chapter to earn your spot among the famous pirates.

The Bounty Hunter: Track down and destroy wanted pirates, accumulating Beli and establishing yourself as the sea's most dreaded scourge. Climb the bounty leaderboards and demonstrate your ability as an outlaw hunter.

Master of Expertise: Unlock all talents and unleash their full potential by reaching the apex of each combat style. Become a master of swordsmanship, a fist-fighting legend, or a gun-slinging gunslinger feared across the archipelago.

Devil Fruit Expert: Understand each Devil Fruit's strengths, weaknesses, and secret combinations. Turn into a walking encyclopedia of fruity abilities, coaching and motivating other pirates on their routes to greatness.

Extraordinary Explorer: Discover Blox Fruits' hidden mysteries. Find Easter eggs, explore hidden areas, and navigate new waterways. Be the first to discover lost riches and cement your position in Blox Fruits mythology.

Conqueror of the Community: Assist and befriend your fellow pirates. Assist newcomers in finding their feet, team up for raids and monsters, and share your expertise. Form relationships with other explorers and make long-lasting memories on the high seas.

Remember, these are only a few of the many challenges and accomplishments that await you. Explore, conquer, and make your imprint on the world of Blox Fruits by embracing the spirit of adventure. Your legend is waiting for you!

www.ingramcontent.com/pod-product-compliance
Lightning Source LLC
LaVergne TN
LVHW051633050326
832903LV00033B/4737